NATIONAL
GEOGRAPHIC

Energized!

Beth Geiger

PICTURE CREDITS
Cover, Thom Lang/Corbis; pages1, 30 (bottom left), 31 (center left), Photodisc Green/
Getty Images; pages 2-3, Ariel Skelley/Corbis; pages 4-5 (center), 34 (second from
bottom), Hughes Martin/Corbis; page 5 (top right), Gunter Marx Photography/Corbis;
pages 5 (center right), 6-7, 8, 30 (top left), 34 (bottom), 35 (second from top), Stone/
Getty Images; page 5 (bottom right), Photodisc Blue/Getty Images; pages 9, 10, 13
(bottom), 25 (bottom left), 28 (bottom left), 31 (center right), 34 (center), Royalty-Free/
Corbis; page 13 (top), Brand X Pictures RF/Getty Images; pages 13 (center), 31 (bottom
left), Herrmann/Starke/Corbis; page 15 (left), Owaki-Kulla/Corbis; page 15 (right),
Mark Richards/Photo Edit; pages 16-17, Paul Steel/Corbis; pages 18-23 (background),
The Image Bank/Getty Images; pages 18, 22-23 (center), Fireworks by Grucci; page 19
(top), Michael Freeman/Corbis; page 19 (bottom), Firefly Productions/Corbis; page 20,
G. Brad Lewis/Photo Researchers, Inc.; page 22 (left), Annebicque Bernard/Corbis
Sygma; page 25 (top left), Neal Preston/Corbis; page 25 (top right), Mike Bluestone/
Photo Researchers, Inc.; pages 25 (bottom right), 31 (bottom right), Photodisc Red/Getty
Images; page 26, 1998 Jeff J. Daly/Fundamental Photographs; page 27 (top right),
Raymond Gehman/National Geographic Image Collection; page 29, W. Cody/Corbis;
pages 30 (top right), 35 (center), Owen Franken/Corbis; page 30 (bottom right), 1988
Richard Megna/Fundamental Photographs; page 31 (top left), William Dow/Corbis;
page 31 (top right), David Grossman/Photo Researchers, Inc.; page 32, David
Stoecklein/Corbis; page 35 (bottom), LWA-Dann Tardif/Corbis; page 36, H&S
Producktion/Corbis.

Produced through the worldwide resources of the National Geographic Society,
John M. Fahey, Jr., President and Chief Executive Officer; Gilbert M. Grosvenor,
Chairman of the Board; Nina D. Hoffman, Executive Vice President and President,
Books and Education Publishing Group.

PREPARED BY NATIONAL GEOGRAPHIC SCHOOL PUBLISHING
Ericka Markman, Senior Vice President and President, Children's Books and
Education Publishing Group; Steve Mico, Senior Vice President, Editorial Director,
Publisher; Francis Downey, Executive Editor; Richard Easby, Editorial Manager; Bea
Jackson, Director of Layout and Design; Jim Hiscott, Design Manager; Cynthia Olson,
Art Director; Margaret Sidlosky, Illustrations Director; Matt Wascavage, Manager of
Publishing Services; Sean Philpotts, Lisa Pergolizzi, Production Managers; Ted Tucker,
Production Specialist.

MANUFACTURING AND QUALITY CONTROL
Christopher A. Liedel, Chief Financial Officer; Phillip L. Schlosser, Director;
Clifton M. Brown III, Manager

CONSULTANT AND REVIEWER
Jordan D. Marché II, Ph.D., University of Wisconsin–Madison

BOOK DEVELOPMENT
Amy Sarver

◀ **Your body uses energy to move.**

Contents

BOOK DESIGN/PHOTO RESEARCH
3R1 Group, Inc.

Copyright © 2006 National Geographic Society.
All Rights Reserved. Reproduction of the whole or any part of the
contents without written permission from the publisher is prohibited.
National Geographic, National Geographic School Publishing,
National Geographic Reading Expeditions, and the Yellow Border
are registered trademarks of the National Geographic Society.

Published by the National Geographic Society
1145 17th Street N.W.
Washington, D.C. 20036-4688

ISBN: 0-7922-5436-8

2010 2009 2008 2007 2006
1 2 3 4 5 6 7 8 9 10 11 12 13 14 15

Printed in Canada.

Energy at Work

▶ Athletes use energy to run.

Energy is all around you. People need energy to run and play. A lamp needs energy to light a room or street. A car needs energy to move down a street. An airplane uses energy to fly through the sky. Energy is the ability to do **work.** Energy makes everything happen.

Look at the pictures.

- What does each picture show?
- How is energy important in each picture?

energy – the ability to do work

work – a force that moves an object over a distance

▲ Lamps use energy to brighten the street.

▲ A car uses energy to move down a street.

▲ An airplane uses energy to fly through the sky.

Big Idea
Energy can change forms.

Set Purpose
Learn what energy is and how it can change forms.

Questions You Will Explore

What is energy?

How do people use energy?

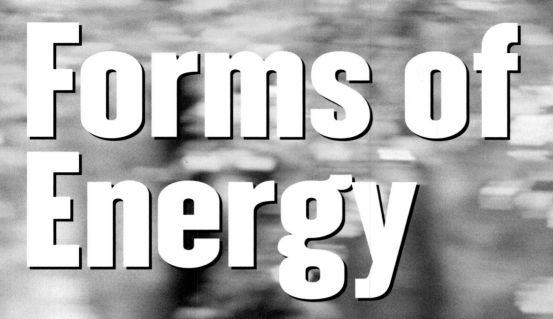

Forms of Energy

Energy is the ability to do work. To understand what work means, you need to know about **force**. A force is a push or a pull. So work is a push or pull that makes an object move. To move an object, you need energy.

force – a push or pull

◄ **The woman uses force to push the stroller.**

Kinetic Energy

There are two main forms of energy. One form is **kinetic energy.** Kinetic energy is the energy of motion. All moving things have kinetic energy. A ball flying through the air has kinetic energy.

kinetic energy – energy of motion

▼ **The ball flying through the air has kinetic energy.**

Potential Energy

The other form of energy is **potential energy.**
Potential energy is energy that is stored. Food
has potential energy. The energy in the food is
stored until your body uses it.

....

potential energy – energy that is stored

▼ **Food has potential energy.**

Heat Energy

Kinetic energy and potential energy come in many forms. For example, heat energy is a form of kinetic energy. Heat energy comes from the movement of tiny particles called **atoms.**

Everything around you is made of atoms. Atoms are always moving. Atoms that move very quickly give off heat energy. Think of a drink. If a drink is hot, its atoms are moving very quickly. The atoms in the drink give off heat energy. In a cold drink, the atoms are moving more slowly. The drink does not give off heat energy.

atom – a tiny particle that makes up all objects

▼ **The moving atoms in a hot drink give off heat energy.**

Electrical Energy

Every day, you use **electrical energy.** This is a form of kinetic energy. Electrical energy is also called electricity.

Wires carry electricity to your home. How does this happen? Electricity is the flow of electrons. Electrons are tiny particles that move around an atom. They also move from one atom to another atom. So electrical energy can move along wires and into your home.

....

electrical energy – energy from moving electrons

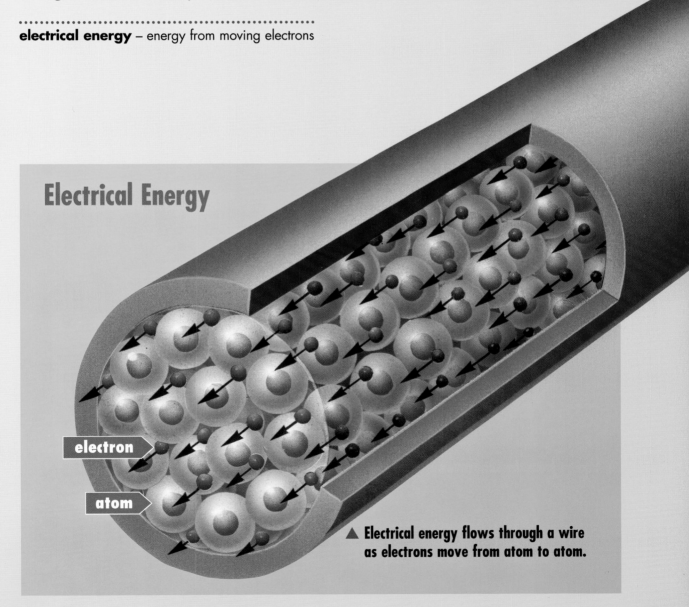

Electrical Energy

electron

atom

▲ Electrical energy flows through a wire as electrons move from atom to atom.

Light Energy

Light energy is another form of kinetic energy. Light energy travels in waves from a light source.

The sun is a source of light. Light from the sun brightens Earth during the day. At night, people use lightbulbs as a source of light.

Light Energy

sun

light waves

▲ **Energy from the sun travels in waves.**

12

Chemical Energy

Chemical energy is potential, or stored, energy. For example, a match has chemical energy. The head of a match is made of chemicals. These chemicals have potential energy. When the match is rubbed, the chemicals catch fire. This releases the energy in the chemicals.

Chemical Energy in a Match

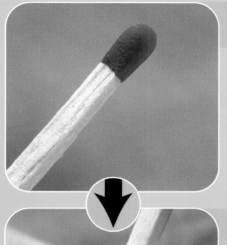

Match Head

The match head is made of chemicals. These chemicals have potential, or stored, energy.

Match Catches Fire

When the match head is rubbed, the chemicals catch fire.

Fire

As the match burns, the chemical energy changes into light and heat energy.

Energy Can Change Forms

Energy does not always stay in one form. It can change from one form to another. Chemical energy in a match can change into light and heat energy. Energy can also change forms when you turn on a lamp. Electrical energy enters the lightbulb. It causes a wire in the bulb to get hot. This wire begins to glow. The glowing wire gives off heat and light energy.

Energy in a Lightbulb

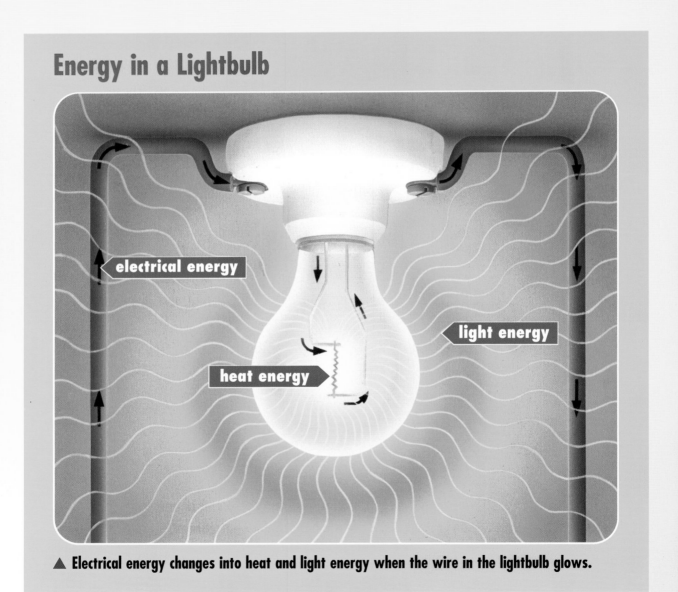

electrical energy

light energy

heat energy

▲ Electrical energy changes into heat and light energy when the wire in the lightbulb glows.

Energy Does Not Disappear

Energy cannot be created or destroyed. It can only change from one form into another. Think about cars and gasoline. Gasoline has chemical energy. A car's engine turns this into kinetic energy. The chemical energy in gasoline does not disappear. It just changes forms. It changes into kinetic energy. This allows the car to move.

Stop and Think!

HOW can energy change forms?

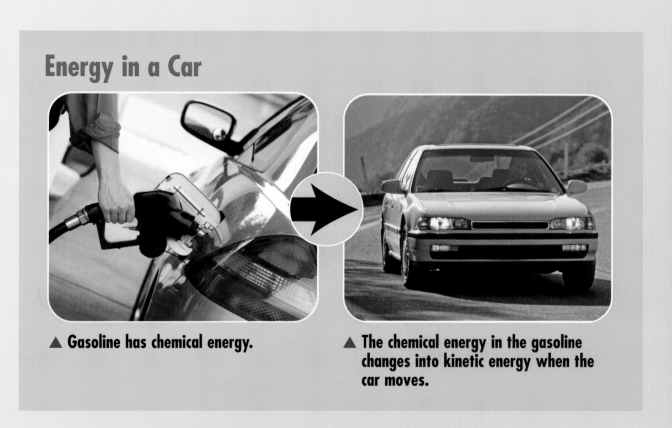

Energy in a Car

▲ Gasoline has chemical energy.

▲ The chemical energy in the gasoline changes into kinetic energy when the car moves.

Recap
Explain how energy can change from one form into another.

Set Purpose
Learn how energy changes forms in fireworks.

Fantastic

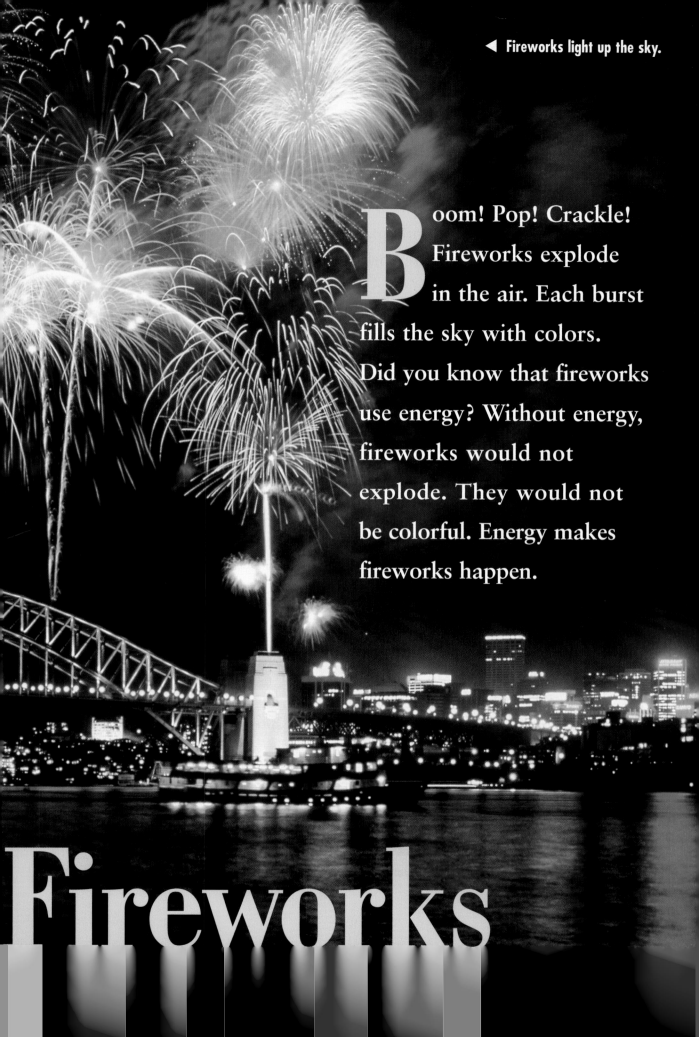

Boom! Pop! Crackle! Fireworks explode in the air. Each burst fills the sky with colors. Did you know that fireworks use energy? Without energy, fireworks would not explode. They would not be colorful. Energy makes fireworks happen.

Fireworks

A Fireworks Family

When fireworks light up the sky, everyone watches. This is especially true for Felix Grucci. Mr. Grucci and his family make fireworks. They make many kinds of fireworks.

▲ The Grucci family makes fireworks.

Changes in the Sky

The Grucci family needs to know a lot of science to make fireworks. Fireworks are made with chemicals. These chemicals explode in the sky.

The chemicals in fireworks have potential, or stored, energy. When the fireworks explode, their potential energy changes into kinetic energy. The chemical energy in the fireworks changes into light and sound energy.

Energy in Fireworks

Chemical Energy
The chemicals in fireworks have potential, or stored, energy.

Light and Sound Energy
When the chemicals catch fire, the potential energy changes into light and sound energy.

Packed With Chemical Energy

Making fireworks is a dangerous job. Why? Fireworks are packed with chemicals that can explode. So the Gruccis are careful.

They start with a **shell.** A shell is a thick tube of paper. The Gruccis place balls of chemicals inside the shell. The balls make the firework colorful when it explodes in the sky.

shell – a thick tube of paper used for making a firework

▼ The balls of chemicals make fireworks colorful when they explode.

Chemicals That Explode

The Gruccis add powder to the shell. The powder is a chemical. It will burst the shell open.

Now the shell is almost ready. What is missing? The **fuse** and the charge! The fuse is a long string. It will burn until the firework is high in the sky. Then it will set fire to the powder and the **bursting charge.** The bursting charge will set the balls of chemicals on fire. It will make them shoot through the sky.

fuse – the part of a firework that sets fire to the powder and bursting charge

bursting charge – the part of a firework that sets fire to the balls of chemicals

Inside a Firework

fuse

powder that explodes

shell

bursting charge

ball of chemicals

▶ A firework is made to explode in the sky.

Into the Sky

Finally, each shell is placed in a thick steel tube on the ground. Ready, set, go! The Gruccis use a computer to launch the shells out of the steel tubes.

The shells fly into the sky. At just the right height, the fireworks explode. The sky fills with color.

▲ Fireworks are launched from steel tubes on the ground.

The Grand Finale!

A firework is an example of how energy changes. The potential, or stored, energy in the firework turns into brilliant shows of light and sound.

The Gruccis use chemical energy to make firework shows for thousands of people. It is a hard job. But the Gruccis love it. They show people how exciting energy can be!

Stop and Think!

HOW can energy change forms in a firework?

◀ **The Gruccis' fireworks explode above the Statue of Liberty.**

Recap

Explain how energy changes forms in fireworks.

Set Purpose

Read these articles to learn more about energy and how it changes forms.

Energy

You cannot see energy. But you can see energy at work. Energy is important to you and everything around you.

Here are some ideas you learned about energy.

- Kinetic energy is energy of motion.
- Potential energy is energy that is stored.
- Energy can change from one form into another.
- Energy cannot be created or destroyed.

Check What You Have Learned

What do the photos show about energy?

▲ A moving ball has kinetic energy.

▲ An apple has potential, or stored, energy.

▲ In a lightbulb, electrical energy changes into heat and light energy.

▲ The energy in gasoline is not created or destroyed. It just changes forms.

▲ **The light from fireflies comes from chemical energy.**

Animal Energy

A firefly is an insect that can make its own light. How does this animal light up? Energy changes forms in its body!

A firefly has special chemicals in its body. The chemicals have potential, or stored, energy. This energy changes forms and becomes light energy. At night, fireflies use their light to signal to each other.

Light for Food

A lot of light energy comes to Earth from the sun. Plants have a special way of storing this energy. Green plants have a chemical called chlorophyll. Chlorophyll can change light from the sun into chemical energy. Plants use this chemical energy for their food.

▲ **Plants use light from the sun to make food.**

▲ **Plants change light energy from the sun into chemical energy for food.**

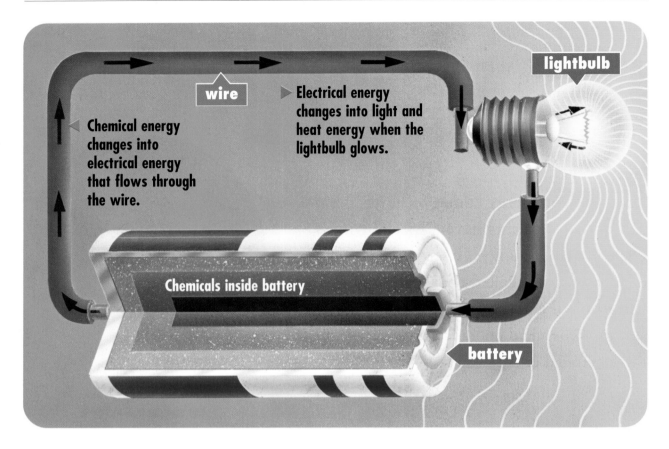

lightbulb

wire

Electrical energy changes into light and heat energy when the lightbulb glows.

Chemical energy changes into electrical energy that flows through the wire.

Chemicals inside battery

battery

Changes in Batteries

▲ A flashlight uses energy stored in batteries.

Batteries contain potential, or stored, energy. This energy is stored in chemicals inside the battery.

Many flashlights use batteries. When you turn a flashlight on, the energy stored in the chemicals changes into electrical energy. This electrical energy flows to the lightbulb. There, the energy changes into heat and light energy. This makes the lightbulb glow.

Nuclear Energy

Nuclear energy is a form of potential energy. It is energy stored in the center of an atom. This stored energy can be released. It is released when the centers of atoms are split apart or joined together. Nuclear power plants split apart the centers of atoms. The nuclear power plants then change this energy into electricity. People use the electricity for power.

▶ **Nuclear power plants change nuclear energy into electricity.**

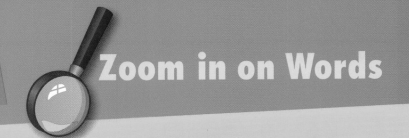
Many kinds of words are used in this book. Here you will learn about adjectives. You will also learn about multiple-meaning words.

Adjectives

Adjectives are words that describe people, places, or things. Find the adjectives below. Then use each adjective in your own sentence.

Kinetic energy is **moving** energy.

Food contains potential, or **stored,** energy.

The atoms in **hot** water move very quickly.

The fireworks are **colorful.**

Multiple-Meaning Words

A multiple-meaning word is a word that has more than one meaning. Find the multiple-meaning words below. Then tell what each multiple-meaning word means.

Plants **store** energy from the sun.

You can buy fruit at the **store.**

Energy can **change** forms.

He holds the **change** in his hands.

The **match** catches fire.

He wants to **match** the colors.

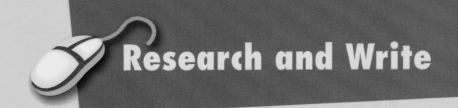

Research and Write

Write About Energy

Pick one form of energy that interests you. Write three questions that you have about that form of energy. Research to find answers to your questions.

Research
Collect books and reference materials, or go online, to find answers to your questions.

Read and Take Notes
As you read, take notes and draw pictures.

Write
Write an answer to each of your three questions. Give facts and details that you learned about the form of energy.

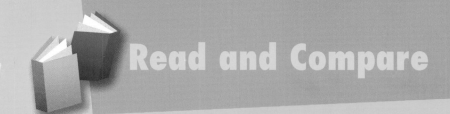
Read More About Energy

Find and read other books about energy. As you read, think about these questions.

- What can energy do?
- How can energy change forms?
- How do scientists learn more about energy?

Books to Read

▲ Read about different forms of energy.

▲ Read about how matter can change.

▲ Read about properties of matter.

Glossary

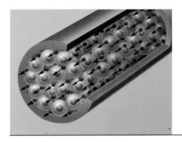

atom (page 10)
A tiny particle that makes up all objects
The electrons in the wire move from atom to atom.

bursting charge (page 21)
The part of a firework that sets fire to the balls of chemicals
The bursting charge causes a firework to explode.

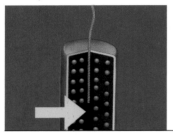

electrical energy (page 11)
Energy from moving electrons
Electrical energy moves through a wire.

KEY CONCEPT

energy (page 4)
The ability to do work
Athletes use energy to run.

KEY CONCEPT

force (page 7)
A push or pull
The woman uses force to push the stroller.

fuse (page 21)

The part of a firework that sets fire to the powder and bursting charge

The fuse burns until the firework reaches the right height in the sky.

kinetic energy (page 8)

Energy of motion

The moving ball has kinetic energy.

potential energy (page 9)

Energy that is stored

Food has potential energy.

shell (page 20)

A thick tube of paper used for making a firework

The firework's shell is packed with chemicals that can explode.

work (page 4)

A force that moves an object over a distance

The man does work as he moves the car.

Index